Cool Jobs

Elizabeth Nonweiler

raintree 🍃

sports coach

make-up artist

cleaner

midwife

crop farmer

teaching assistant

graphic artist

runway model

merchant

news reporter

astronomer

lawyer

Interesting facts about the pictures

page 2: A **sports coach** helps players develop skills, play fairly, keep safe and enjoy sport. Football coaches make game plans and decide which players will play in which positions.

page 3: A **make-up artist** designs and puts on make-up for actors and models. Make-up helps an actor to be seen or changes the actor. This artist is changing an actor to look like a clown.

page 4: **Cleaners** keep buildings clean. This is especially important in hospitals and where there is food, because dirt can spread diseases. They may use machines like this floor scrubber.

page 5: **Midwives** look after mothers when they are going to have a baby, when their babies are born and for a few weeks after. They give parents advice about how to look after babies.

page 6: **Crop farmers** manage farms that grow crops such as maize. They must know about soil, plants, insects and how to run a business. They have to operate machines in all weathers.

page 7: **Teaching assistants** help teachers in the classroom. They may teach small groups of children, help children who find something difficult or help teachers get lessons ready.

page 8: **Graphic artists** put pictures and writing together for leaflets, advertisements, book illustrations, business cards or websites. They draw their designs or use a graphic tablet.

page 9: **Runway models** walk, turn and stand still on a platform called a runway, or catwalk, to show off clothes for fashion designers. They have to keep changing clothes and make-up.

page 10: **Merchants** buy things from people who make them and sell them to people who want them. They sell from shops, street markets, supermarkets or the internet. This is a bicycle shop.

page 11: **News reporters** collect news and write or speak about it. They may interview people, take photographs or film what they see and hear. They try to explain clearly what they find out.

page 12: **Astronomers** study moons, planets, stars and galaxies. They use telescopes, special cameras and computers. Then they write and tell people about what they have discovered.

page 13: **Lawyers** study the laws (rules) of a country. They explain a law when someone is accused of breaking it, to help make sure what happens to that person is fair.

Letter-sound correspondences

Level 2 books cover the following letter-sound correspondences.
Letter-sound correspondences highlighted in green can be found in this book.

ant	**b**ig	**c**at	**d**og	**e**gg	**f**ish	**g**et	**h**ot	**i**t
jet	**k**ey	**l**et	**m**an	**n**ut	**o**ff	**p**an	**qu**een	**r**un
sun	**t**ap	**u**p	**v**an	**w**et	bo**x**	**y**es	**z**oo	
du**ck**	fi**sh**	**ch**ips	si**ng**	**th**in **th**is	k**ee**p	l**oo**k m**oo**n	**ar**t	c**or**n

s**ay**	b**oy**	r**ai**n	**oi**l	b**oa**t	**ea**t	p**ie**	h**igh**
m**a**k**e**	th**e**s**e**	l**i**k**e**	n**o**t**e**	fl**u**t**e** t**u**b**e**	**ou**t	s**aw**	**au**thor
h**er**	b**ir**d	t**ur**n	**air**port	fl**ew** st**ew**	bl**ue** c**ue**	**ph**one	**wh**en